SCHOLASTIC

INFERENCES & DRAWING CONCLUSIONS

by Linda Ward Beech

NEW YORK • TORONTO • LONDON • AUCKLAND • SYDNEY
MEXICO CITY • NEW DELHI • HONG KONG • BUENOS AIRES

Teaching *Resources*

Cover design by Maria Lilja
Interior design by Sydney Wright
Interior illustrations by Mike Gordon

ISBN-13 978-0-439-55411-4
ISBN-10 0-439-55411-X

17 18 19 20   40   14 13

Contents

Introduction

Reading comprehension involves numerous thinking skills. Among these skills is a reader's facility at making inferences and drawing conclusions, at deriving meaning from language with layers of implied meaning. The reader who is adept at making inferences and the related skill of drawing conclusions gains a richer and deeper understanding of a text. In this book, you'll find that Exercises 1–17 help students practice the skill of making inferences. Exercises 18–35 focus on practice with drawing conclusions. Use pages 8 and 9 after you introduce the skills to give students help in understanding them.

Using This Book

Pages 8–9

After introducing the concepts of making inferences and drawing conclusions to students (see pages 6 and 7), duplicate and pass out pages 8 and 9. Use page 8 to help students review what they have learned about making inferences. By explaining their thinking, students are using metacognition to analyze how they recognized and utilized these clues. Page 9 helps students review what they have learned about drawing conclusions.

Pages 10–26

These pages provide practice in making inferences. To begin, students read a paragraph. The first question asks students to distinguish facts from inferences. The second question requires students to make an inference of their own regarding the passage they read. If students disagree with a given answer, encourage them to explain their thinking. Accept all reasonable responses.

Pages 27–44

These pages provide practice in drawing conclusions. To get started, students read a paragraph. The first question requires students to practice drawing a conclusion rooted in evidence from the text. The second question invites students to recognize that some information may not be presented in the text. For both of these multiple-choice questions, students must choose the answer that best completes the sentence.

Pages 45–46

After they have completed the practice pages, use these pages to assess students' progress.

Page 47

You may wish to keep a record of students' progress as they complete the practice pages. Sample comments that will help you guide students to improving skills might include:

- reads carelessly
- misunderstands text
- is unmindful of the author's point of view
- does not apply prior knowledge
- overlooks clues
- has difficulty visualizing

Teaching How to Make Inferences

1. Introduce the concept: Write this sentence on the board.

Walker received a funny e-mail from his friend Lily.

Ask students which of the following sentences goes best with the statement.

　　A. Walker will write back to Lily.

　　B. Walker will buy something on the Internet.

2. Model thinking: Think aloud as you guide students in identifying **A.** as the sentence that best goes with the statement.

Most people respond to e-mails from friends. I know this because that's what my friends and I do. Since the e-mail from Lily was funny, Walker will probably mention something about that when he answers her.

Although Walker could buy something while he's on the Internet, there's nothing in the sentence that suggests he will.

3. Define the skill: Tell students that a writer doesn't always explain every fact or detail about something. A writer expects that readers will fill in missing information from their own experience. Readers do this by putting together what they already know and what they have read to make the best guess they can. When readers add information from their own experience to what is stated in a text, they are making an inference. Point out that students make inferences all the time, not only in their reading but in other ways as well. For example, people make inferences when they look at a photograph or see someone walking by on the street.

Scholastic Teaching Resources　*Inferences & Drawing Conclusions*

Teaching How to Draw Conclusions

1. Introduce the concept: Write these sentences on the board.

Judd likes the color blue.

He says it gives him a peaceful feeling.

Judd bought paint for his living room.

Ask students what color paint they think Judd might have bought.

2. Model thinking: Think aloud as you guide students in recognizing that these sentences, while sharing information about Judd, help the reader come to the conclusion that Judd might have bought blue paint.

The first sentence states that Judd likes the color blue. The second sentence explains why Judd prefers blue. People generally like their living rooms to be peaceful colors. These are good clues about what color paint Judd might have bought for his living room.

3. Define the skill: Tell students that a conclusion is a decision that readers make after thinking about the information in a text. Since a writer doesn't always state all of his or her ideas, readers often have to look for clues to understand the whole passage, paragraph, or story. Readers must put together the clues that the writer provides and then draw the best conclusions they can to understand the text. Caution students that a conclusion should make sense.

Learning Page

What Is an Inference?

When you read a passage, you are not always given every fact or detail. How does a reader learn what this unstated information is? One way is by making inferences. A reader might think:

What else do I know about this subject? How does what I know fit with what I have read?

These questions help a reader make an **inference**. An inference is a kind of guess made after thinking about what you have read and what you already know.

Read this passage.

Mummies—the preserved bodies of the dead—were made at least 7,000 years ago in Chile by the Chinchorro people. The Inca of Peru also made mummies of their dead kings about 3,000 years ago. In ancient China, people tried to preserve emperors in suits made of jade. Of course, the best-known mummy makers were the early Egyptians, who spent up to 70 days preparing a body.

Find the facts in the passage. Complete these sentences to write four facts from the passage.

1 The Chinchorro _People from Chile_____.

2 The Inca _____.

3 The Chinese _____.

4 The Egyptians _____.

Now think about how people today honor the dead. Then recall the facts in the passage. Make an inference. How might ancient people have felt about the dead?

My Inference: _____

_____

Scholastic Teaching Resources   Inferences & Drawing Conclusions

What Is a Conclusion?

When you read a passage, you often have to be a detective. You have to find ideas that the writer does not always state. How does a reader do this? One way is by looking for clues and putting them together to draw a conclusion. A reader might think:

What clues—facts and details—has the writer given me? How can I use these clues to make a decision about what the writer is telling me?

These questions help a reader draw a **conclusion**. A conclusion is a decision a reader makes after considering all the information given.

Read this passage.

Corn comes from the maize plant and is grown in many parts of the world. Some kinds of corn are grown as animal feed while other kinds are raised as food for people. In the summertime, many Americans enjoy corn on the cob. Corn is used in many other forms as well. Supermarkets sell cereals made from corn, frozen corn kernels, canned corn, corn oil, cornstarch, cornmeal, corn chips, and popcorn. Corn is also used to make foods such as tacos and muffins.

Answer these questions to identify clues in the passage.

1 Where is corn grown? _____

2 Who or what eats corn? _____

3 What are some corn products? _____

4 What are some foods that contain corn? _____

Now draw a conclusion. What can you conclude about corn?

My Conclusion: _____

_____

Making Inferences

Read the paragraph. Answer the questions.

In 1829, Daniel Webster started a page program
in the United States Senate. The pages are young
people who work for the senators. For example,
pages run errands and deliver messages. Pages
are chosen by the senators of their home states.
They must be 16 years old, have good grades,
and show leadership qualities. Pages live
near the Capitol Building and attend school.
They are excused from homework when the senators work overtime. Pages
get paid, but the biggest reward is the experience of working in the Senate.

1 Fill in the correct circle to show whether each statement is a fact or an inference.

Fact   Inference

Fact	Inference	
⊘	◯	Pages run errands for senators.
◯	⊘	Pages are interested in government.
⊘	◯	Pages go to school.
◯	⊘	It is an honor to be a Senate page.

2 Write **yes** or **no** under each heading on the chart to show if the word describes
a Senate page.

Busy	Responsible	Lazy
Y	Y	N

Scholastic Teaching Resources   Inferences & Drawing Conclusions

Making Inferences

Read the paragraph. Answer the questions.

Have you ever heard of a walking school bus? Students in some parts of the United States travel by such buses every day. The "driver" of these buses is often a parent who leads a group to and from school—on foot. If the group is large, there is usually another adult who acts as the "conductor" and walks at the rear of the group to make sure that everyone stays together. Students are picked up and dropped off at their homes. Walking buses help students get fresh air, and they also help reduce pollution and traffic congestion.

SCHOOL CROSSING

1 Fill in the correct circle to show whether each statement is a fact or an inference.

Fact   Inference

○   ⊗   Walking school buses provide good exercise.

⊗   ○   Two adults usually accompany a large group.

○   ⊗   Slow walkers could cause problems for a group.

○   ⊗   Walking buses aren't much fun in bad weather.

2 Write **yes** or **no** under each heading on the chart to show if the word describes a walking school bus.

Healthy	Unsafe	Expensive
Y	N	N

Making Inferences

Read the paragraph. Answer the questions.

You've heard of recycling, but do you know about freecycling? When you freecycle, you give away things you no longer want or need. Freecyclers can also acquire things that someone else is getting rid of. Lists of things available for freecycling and lists of things wanted by freecyclers are posted on Web sites. People who sign up and find just what they want then arrange to pick up the items. Some popular items for freecyclers are bicycles, exercise equipment, furniture, and computer parts.

1 Fill in the correct circle to show whether each statement is a fact or an inference.

Fact **Inference**

○ ⊗ Freecycling is handy if you are cleaning a garage.

○ ⊘ You could furnish a room from freecycled things.

⊘ ○ Computer parts are favorite recycled items.

○ ⊘ It's easiest to freecycle with people who are nearby.

2 Write **yes** or **no** under each heading on the chart to show if the word describes freecycling.

Costly	Dishonest	Useful
N	N	Y

Scholastic Teaching Resources   Inferences & Drawing Conclusions

Making Inferences

Read the paragraph. Answer the questions.

NASCAR is the National Association for Stock Car Racing. In recent years, this organization has made some changes in its rules. For example, steel and foam cushioning has been placed around NASCAR tracks to better absorb impact from hurtling cars. Race car drivers must now wear special head restraints that limit their neck movement during sudden stops. Air filters have been added to race cars to keep carbon monoxide out of the cockpit. The tires also have straps now to keep the wheels from flying off during crashes.

1 Fill in the correct circle to show whether each statement is a fact or an inference.

Fact   Inference

◯   ◯   NASCAR's new rules were made to improve safety.

◯   ◯   Drivers now wear head restraints.

◯   ◯   Race car drivers are sometimes hurt in accidents.

◯   ◯   Race cars give off carbon monoxide.

2 Write **yes** or **no** under each heading on the chart to show if the word describes stock car racing.

Unregulated	Safety Conscious	Dangerous

Making Inferences

Read the paragraph. Answer the questions.

When they come to a stoplight, drivers sometimes look at the people in other cars. Mr. Beren noticed that a man in the car next to him had a large green parrot on the passenger seat. The parrot seemed to be talking. When the man rolled down his window, Mr. Beren was surprised to hear that the bird wasn't talking but barking. The owner leaned out his window and explained, "He lives with three golden retrievers, and he thinks he's a dog." The light changed, and Mr. Beren smiled all the way home.

1 Fill in the correct circle to show whether each statement is a fact or an inference.

Fact   Inference

◯   ◯   Mr. Beren noticed a large green parrot in a car.

◯   ◯   Mr. Beren was curious.

◯   ◯   The parrot learned to bark by listening to the dogs.

◯   ◯   The parrot's behavior amused Mr. Beren.

2 Write **yes** or **no** under each heading on the chart to show if the word describes Mr. Beren's reaction.

Tickled	Disapproving	Uninterested

Making Inferences

Read the paragraph. Answer the questions.

Great Zimbabwe, a ruins located within the African country of Zimbabwe, was a center of trade from the late thirteenth century to the middle of the fifteenth century. It was also the home of powerful rulers. Today, scientists are studying the walls found among the ruins. They are made of smooth granite and are about 35 feet high and 16 feet deep. No mortar or plaster was used in building them. Some archaeologists believe that the walls were built not for defense but to inspire awe toward the rulers.

1 Fill in the correct circle to show whether each statement is a fact or an inference.

Fact   Inference

◯   ◯   Great Zimbabwe is located in Africa.

◯   ◯   Great Zimbabwe is a place of historic value.

◯   ◯   The builders of the walls were skilled.

◯   ◯   The walls of Great Zimbabwe reach 35 feet high.

2 Write **yes** or **no** under each heading on the chart to show if the word describes Great Zimbabwe.

Fascinating	Polluted	Ancient

EXERCISE

7

Making Inferences

Read the paragraph. Answer the questions.

During the Ice Age many, many thousands of years ago, people depended on the animals they hunted. Not only did they need these animals for food, but the hunters used them to make clothing, tools, and other necessities. Ancient paintings found in caves show us what these animals were like. Some were huge, such as the woolly mammoth and the woolly rhinoceros. Other animals that inspired Ice Age artists still exist today. These include bison, horses, musk ox, and deer.

1 Fill in the correct circle to show whether each statement is a fact or an inference.

Fact   Inference

○   ○   Some Ice Age animals are now extinct.

○   ○   Ice Age artists were good observers of animals.

○   ○   Some Ice Age paintings show bison and horses.

○   ○   Animals were very important to Ice Age people.

2 Write **yes** or **no** under each heading on the chart to show if the word describes life in the Ice Age.

Glamorous	Modern	Hard

Scholastic Teaching Resources   Inferences & Drawing Conclusions

Making Inferences

Read the paragraph. Answer the questions.

Who was one of the finest architects during Thomas Jefferson's time? The answer is Thomas Jefferson. He became a skilled draftsman as a boy. One of his first projects was to plan his own home. He started designing in 1767 and began building in 1770. Jefferson called this place Monticello, and he lived there until his death in 1826. Jefferson also helped plan the new U.S. capital, Washington, D.C. He was the first president to be inaugurated in that city. In later years, he helped design the handsome buildings at the University of Virginia.

1 Fill in the correct circle to show whether each statement is a fact or an inference.

Fact   Inference

◯   ◯   Jefferson was a man of many talents.

◯   ◯   Monticello was Jefferson's home.

◯   ◯   Jefferson helped plan the University of Virginia.

◯   ◯   Jefferson learned his drafting skills while young.

2 Write **yes** or **no** under each heading on the chart to show if the word describes Thomas Jefferson as an architect.

Industrious	Committed	Talented

Name _____ Date _____

Making Inferences

Read the paragraph. Answer the questions.

Prairie dogs are not really dogs; they're rodents. However, like canines, prairie dogs communicate by barking. Many of the sounds they make alert their colony to danger. For example, prairie dogs have one call for coyotes and another for hawks. When a coyote is sighted, other prairie dogs pop up from their burrows to keep track of where it goes. If a hawk is signaled, they dive into their burrows. Prairie dogs make still other sounds when humans are near. Most surprisingly, prairie dogs have distinct calls for different kinds of real dogs.

1 Fill in the correct circle to show whether each statement is a fact or an inference.

Fact   **Inference**

◯   ◯   Prairie dogs are actually rodents.

◯   ◯   Hawks are bigger threats than coyotes.

◯   ◯   Prairie dogs make barking sounds.

◯   ◯   Prairie dogs have special calls for people.

2 Write **yes** or **no** under each heading on the chart to show if the word describes prairie dog communications.

Watchful	Unpleasant	Silent

Making Inferences

Read the paragraph. Answer the questions.

Many people put flowers in a vase, but in Japan arranging flowers is considered an art. It is called *ikebana* and has been practiced for about 500 years. Japanese teens often study flower arranging in school, and professional arrangers spend years learning the art. Only a few flowers are used in an arrangement. These are carefully chosen to make a graceful composition. The tallest flower represents heaven, the shortest flower is for earth, and the one in the middle stands for humans. Most homes in Japan have a special place where flower arrangements are displayed.

1 Fill in the correct circle to show whether each statement is a fact or an inference.

Fact   **Inference**

◯   ◯   Ikebana reflects an appreciation of beauty.

◯   ◯   The Japanese have practiced ikebana for 500 years.

◯   ◯   Much thought goes into a Japanese arrangement.

◯   ◯   Students learn about ikebana in school.

2 Write **yes** or **no** under each heading on the chart to show if the word describes ikebana.

Careless	Elegant	Meaningful

Making Inferences

Read the paragraph. Answer the questions.

Did you know that monadnocks and inselbergs are similar? They are both landforms of isolated rock mountains that stand higher than a surrounding region. Because of their rock composition, monadnocks and inselbergs are not much affected by erosion. *Monadnock* is from a word in the Algonquin language that was given to a mass of rock in New Hampshire called Mt. Monadnock. The rock mountains called inselbergs tower above plains in tropical areas such as central Nigeria in Africa.

1 Fill in the correct circle to show whether each statement is a fact or an inference.

Fact   Inference

◯   ◯   Monadnocks have a different appearance than other mountains.

◯   ◯   Inselbergs are like rock islands that rise over flat land.

◯   ◯   Monadnocks and inselbergs are composed of rock.

◯   ◯   The Algonquins lived in what is now New Hampshire.

2 Write **yes** or **no** under each heading on the chart to show if the word describes monadnocks.

Unusual Looking	Green	Level

Scholastic Teaching Resources   *Inferences & Drawing Conclusions*

Making Inferences

Read the paragraph. Answer the questions.

The organizers of the Olympics face many problems. One of the biggest is often the weather. In the years 1932, 1956, and 1964, a lack of snow made things difficult at the Winter Olympics. Scorching temperatures during some Summer Olympics have also caused problems. In 1924, only half of the runners in a cross-country event made it to the finish line because of the heat. Other weather-related problems have created headaches, too. In 1896 in Greece, the rowing races had to be cancelled because the sea was too rough. A flood once almost halted the Olympics in Paris.

1 Fill in the correct circle to show whether each statement is a fact or an inference.

Fact   Inference

○   ○   A lack of snow has threatened the Winter Olympics.

○   ○   Weather conditions affect the Olympic Games.

○   ○   Olympic organizers have to be good problem solvers.

○   ○   High temperatures can be a problem in the Summer Games.

2 Write **yes** or **no** under each heading on the chart to show if the word describes how weather affects the Olympics.

Unpredictable	Boring	Challenging

Name _____   Date _____

Making Inferences

Read the paragraph. Answer the questions.

It's fast, strong, and a very good hunter.
It can catch sand rats, jerboas, and ground
squirrels. It is also known for its jumping
skills, which it uses when hunting birds.
What is this animal? It's the caracal, a cat
that lives in the deserts of Africa, the
Middle East, and parts of Asia. The caracal
has short, sleek hair that is reddish-brown in color. Its large, pointed ears are
black on the back. Usually, the caracal does its hunting at night to avoid the hot
temperatures of the desert in daytime.

1 Fill in the correct circle to show whether each statement is a fact or an inference.

Fact   Inference

○   ○   The caracal is a wild animal.

○   ○   Temperatures in the desert drop at night.

○   ○   The caracal can jump when catching birds.

○   ○   The caracal is a carnivore.

2 Write **yes** or **no** under each heading on the chart to show if the word correctly

describes the caracal.

Sweet	Predator	Fragile

Scholastic Teaching Resources   *Inferences & Drawing Conclusions*

Making Inferences

Read the paragraph. Answer the questions.

Long ago, there were no clocks or watches. People had to figure out ways to mark the passing of time. In about 870 A.D., King Alfred of England invented a candle clock. He used candles that were 12 inches long and marked them off in equal sections. To keep air drafts from affecting how the candle burned, he created a lantern to fit over the candle. People could then measure time by noting how long a section of the candle took to burn. The problem with candle clocks? They kept burning up!

1 Fill in the correct circle to show whether each statement is a fact or an inference.

Fact   Inference

○   ○   King Alfred of England invented the candle clock.

○   ○   People had to keep replacing the candles.

○   ○   The candle clock had a lantern over it.

○   ○   Rooms in 870 A.D. were probably drafty.

2 Write **yes** or **no** under each heading on the chart to show if the word describes the candle clock.

Clever	Permanent	Accurate

Making Inferences

Read the paragraph. Answer the questions.

Emperor penguin parents share the responsibilities of caring for their offspring. The female lays one egg, which she places on the male's feet. He keeps the egg between the top of his feet and a special fold of skin on his tummy. He is careful not to drop the egg. While the female goes back to the sea, the father huddles on the ice with other dads for two months. The males do not eat during this time. The female returns when the egg is ready to hatch. She feeds the chick a meal of fish. The male goes to find food in the sea for himself and the chick. Both parents then share the work of feeding the chick.

1 Fill in the correct circle to show whether each statement is a fact or an inference.

Fact **Inference**

◯ ◯ A female emperor penguin lays one egg at a time.

◯ ◯ The male keeps the egg until it is ready to hatch.

◯ ◯ The male keeps the egg safe and warm.

◯ ◯ The male is hungry by the time the chick hatches.

2 Write **yes** or **no** under each heading on the chart to show if the word describes penguin parents.

Impatient	Selfish	Dutiful

Scholastic Teaching Resources *Inferences & Drawing Conclusions*

Making Inferences

Read the paragraph. Answer the questions.

Have you ever noticed how some words are used together all the time? It's as if they were partners. For example, people often say "mix and match" or "nuts and bolts." Other words that are often paired are "kiss and tell," "wash and dry," and "meat and potatoes." Perhaps you have used a few of these phrases, too. How many times have you said you were "sick and tired" of something? Have you ever ordered food that was "sweet and sour"? And no doubt you've spent time most days putting on your "socks and shoes."

mix and match

1 Fill in the correct circle to show whether each statement is a fact or an inference.

Fact   **Inference**

◯   ◯   An example of paired words is "meat and potatoes."

◯   ◯   People get in the habit of using certain words together.

◯   ◯   The words "socks and shoes" are often used together.

◯   ◯   Words used together have a catchy sound.

2 Write **yes** or **no** under each heading on the chart to show if the word describes words used together.

Unexpected	Lucky	Common

Making Inferences

Read the paragraph. Answer the questions.

When the calendar says April 1, be careful! Someone may play a silly joke on you because it is April Fool's Day. This day is celebrated in the United States, France, England, and Scotland. Putting salt in the sugar bowl is a popular trick in the U.S. A prank people use in France is to pin a paper fish on someone else's back without getting caught. The person wearing the fish is called a *poisson d'avril*, or April fish. In England, a person who is tricked is called a *noddie* or a *gawby*. An April fool in Scotland is a *cuckoo* or a *gowk*.

1 Fill in the correct circle to show whether each statement is a fact or an inference.

Fact   **Inference**

○   ○   April Fool's is on the first day of April.

○   ○   A paper fish prank is popular in France.

○   ○   A noddie or a gawby is an English April fool.

○   ○   People enjoy playing silly tricks on others.

2 Write **yes** or **no** under each heading on the chart to show if the word describes April Fool's Day.

Mean	Good-Natured	Serious

Drawing Conclusions

Read the paragraph. Answer the questions.

What's the secret of a winning cyclist? Skill, daring, and good preparation do make a difference, of course, but another answer is technology. Since bicycle races are often very close, riders need every advantage they can get. For instance, a racer might wear a suit designed so that it has no creases or wrinkles to affect the airflow. Special racing shoes are covered with a seamless silver fabric for the same reason. Aerodynamic brakes and a bike frame made to cut through the air effectively are also part of a racer's equipment.

Choose the answer that best completes each sentence.

1 From this paragraph you can conclude that

Ⓐ cyclists like to look good when racing.

Ⓑ many riders wear the wrong kind of clothing.

Ⓒ air resistance affects a rider's speed.

Ⓓ some riders don't spend enough time training.

2 From the paragraph you **cannot** tell

Ⓐ what materials are used in making racing bikes.

Ⓑ that riders need every advantage they can get.

Ⓒ that bicycle races are often very close.

Ⓓ that riders must have skill to win a race.

Drawing Conclusions

Read the paragraph. Answer the questions.

Veterans Day is celebrated on November 11. It honors
soldiers who fought in wars for the United States.
Observances take place all over the country. Some
are held on battleships or at military bases. Others
take place in cemeteries, churches, or government
buildings. People give speeches, march in parades,
and say prayers. For many people, red poppies are a symbol of Veterans Day.
These flowers once grew on the battlefields of Europe during World War I
(1914–1918) and are now symbols of the blood shed there and in other places.

Choose the answer that best completes each sentence.

1 From this paragraph you can conclude that

Ⓐ Veterans Day is a time of joyful feasting.

Ⓑ most battles happen on fields of flowers.

Ⓒ few communities celebrate Veterans Day.

Ⓓ Veterans Day is a sad time for some people.

2 From the paragraph you **cannot** tell

Ⓐ why poppies are a symbol of Veterans Day.

Ⓑ how many people have been lost in wars.

Ⓒ how people observe Veterans Day.

Ⓓ what month Veterans Day occurs in.

Drawing Conclusions

Read the paragraph. Answer the questions.

Elephants don't usually dress up, but some clothing designers thought that these large animals could be quite fashionable. So the designers made some oversize outfits such as tweed suits, a cloak, and some dresses. They even included gigantic earrings and shoes. The designers had to use stepladders to get their models dressed, but the elephants were very well behaved. When all was ready, a photographer took pictures for a fashion magazine. The money the elephants made from their modeling was donated to some elephant causes.

Choose the answer that best completes each sentence.

1 From this paragraph you can conclude that

Ⓐ elephants enjoy reading fashion magazines.

Ⓑ the clothing designers wanted to get attention.

Ⓒ many people bought the elephant clothes.

Ⓓ the elephants often work as fashion models.

2 From the paragraph you **cannot** tell

Ⓐ how the elephants' earnings were used.

Ⓑ why the designers made elephant clothes.

Ⓒ what color clothes the elephants modeled.

Ⓓ how the elephants acted when they were dressed.

Drawing Conclusions

Read the paragraph. Answer the questions.

Most trees have leaves growing from their branches, but a cottonwood tree along U.S. Highway 50 near Middle Gate, Nevada, has something else. Hanging from the branches of this tree are shoes. High heels, work boots, flip-flops, baby booties, sandals, running shoes, even snorkeling flippers all dangle from this tree. Some people buy shoes just to put in the tree. Others take them as needed. To the people who live in the area, the tree is a symbol of charity and decency. Many passersby have benefited from its unusual and useful offerings.

Choose the answer that best completes each sentence.

1 From this paragraph you can conclude that

  Ⓐ flip-flips are the most popular footwear in the tree.

  Ⓑ the shoes fall from the tree when autumn comes.

  Ⓒ people living nearby are proud of the tree.

  Ⓓ most of the shoes are worn and old and unusable.

2 From the paragraph you **cannot** tell

  Ⓐ where the cottonwood tree with shoes is located.

  Ⓑ why some of the shoes in the tree are new.

  Ⓒ what kinds of shoes are found in the tree.

  Ⓓ how the tradition of a tree with shoes got started.

Scholastic Teaching Resources   Inferences & Drawing Conclusions

EXERCISE

22

Drawing Conclusions

Read the paragraph. Answer the questions.

When she was young, Madame C. J. Walker's hair began
falling out. She tried a lot of remedies, but none helped.
So she invented her own mixture—and it worked. Soon
after, she decided to start her own hair-care business. At
first, she sold her products door-to-door. Then she began
selling products by mail. Madame Walker set up factories and opened beauty
parlors in many cities. She also started training schools for her workers. By the
time of her death in 1919, 25,000 women worked for Madame Walker. She was
the first black female millionaire. Much of her wealth went to help others.

Choose the answer that best completes each sentence.

1 From this paragraph you can conclude that

   Ⓐ Madame C. J. Walker was a good businesswoman.

   Ⓑ Madame Walker's products were very expensive.

   Ⓒ no one used hair products before Madame Walker.

   Ⓓ most hair products today are sold door-to-door.

2 From the paragraph you **cannot** tell

   Ⓐ why Madame Walker invented a hair product.

   Ⓑ what Madame Walker did with her money.

   Ⓒ what ingredients were used in the hair products.

   Ⓓ how Madame Walker sold her hair-care treatments.

Drawing Conclusions

Read the paragraph. Answer the questions.

The Chinese learned to make silk cloth almost 5,000 years
ago. At that time, they were the only ones who knew how
to make it. Soon traders from China found that people in
the West would pay great prices for silk. So traders traveled
long distances on camels across harsh deserts and over
high mountains to sell their silk. They also brought styles of art and Chinese
inventions such as gunpowder to the West. They returned with gold, nuts,
perfumes, and goods from the West. This trade route became known as the
Silk Route. Many of the stopping places on the route became great cities.

Choose the answer that best completes each sentence.

1 From this paragraph you can conclude that

Ⓐ travel on the Silk Route was safe and easy.

Ⓑ gunpowder was an unimportant Chinese invention.

Ⓒ ideas were also exchanged along the Silk Route.

Ⓓ prices charged in the West for silk were too high.

2 From the paragraph you **cannot** tell

Ⓐ what kind of land the Silk Route crossed.

Ⓑ the names of some of the cities along the Silk Route.

Ⓒ what goods from the West traders brought to China.

Ⓓ when the Chinese first began making silk.

Scholastic Teaching Resources   Inferences & Drawing Conclusions

Drawing Conclusions

Read the paragraph. Answer the questions.

What is letterboxing? It's a hobby that has grown in popularity in recent years. To get started you need a notebook, an ink pad, a compass, and good walking shoes. Most people check a Web site to obtain clues telling how to find letterboxes. Each letterbox is a container holding a rubber stamp and a notebook. Letterboxes are hidden in public places such as parks or woods. When seekers find a letterbox, they add its stamp to their notebook. Most letterbox fans also carry their own stamps, which they stamp into the notebook in the letterbox. This is called "stamping in."

Choose the answer that best completes each sentence.

1 From this paragraph you can conclude that

Ⓐ everyone enjoys the hobby of letterboxing.

Ⓑ letterboxing is an ancient tradition.

Ⓒ people trespass a lot when letterboxing.

Ⓓ letterboxing is like an outdoor detective game.

2 From the paragraph you **cannot** tell

Ⓐ what people will find in a letterbox.

Ⓑ how many letterboxes exist in the United States.

Ⓒ where people go to find the clues for letterboxing.

Ⓓ what equipment you need for letterboxing.

Drawing Conclusions

Read the paragraph. Answer the questions.

Today, many hubcaps are made of plastic, but not so long ago, they were made from stamped metal. These earlier hubcaps featured all kinds of designs. Wreaths, emblems, crests, spokes, and geometric patterns were popular. Some hubcap designers became quite well known. Today, these hubcaps of the past are collectors' items. Some are exhibited in hubcap museums; others are part of private collections. A ranch displaying hubcaps in California has even become recognized as a state historical landmark because of its "twentieth century folk art environment."

Choose the answer that best completes each sentence.

1 From this paragraph you can conclude that

(A) everyone wants to collect old hubcaps.

(B) today's cars lack interesting hubcaps.

(C) hubcap designers made a lot of money.

(D) hubcaps often fall off car wheels.

2 From the paragraph you **cannot** tell

(A) what kinds of designs hubcaps have featured.

(B) what material was used in earlier hubcaps.

(C) who the collectors of old hubcaps are.

(D) why a hubcap ranch is a state landmark.

Scholastic Teaching Resources   Inferences & Drawing Conclusions

Name _____ Date _____

Drawing Conclusions

Read the paragraph. Answer the questions.

The phone at a zoo in Scotland kept ringing, but no one spoke when the employees answered. The only sound was a kind of snuffling noise. This went on for two nights. Everyone was mystified. Then an employee found the prankster. It was Chippy, an 11-year-old chimp who had snatched a cell phone from one of his keepers. To make his calls, Chippy had been hitting the "redial" button. Thanks to Chippy's cellular monkey business, the zookeeper's phone bill was rather high that month! Since then, the keeper stores his cell phone in a deep pocket.

Choose the answer that best completes each sentence.

1 From this paragraph you can conclude that

Ⓐ Chippy was playing with the cell phone.

Ⓑ Chippy wanted to scare the zoo employees.

Ⓒ Chippy had to pay for all the calls he made.

Ⓓ Chippy knew the telephone number of the zoo.

2 From the paragraph you **cannot** tell

Ⓐ how Chippy got the cell phone.

Ⓑ how long Chippy had the cell phone.

Ⓒ where the keeper stores his phone now.

Ⓓ what other pranks Chippy has pulled.

Name _____   Date _____

Drawing Conclusions

Read the paragraph. Answer the questions.

Passing motorists often think they have stumbled onto a huge art installation. Instead, they are going by a testing ground for a paint company. About 20,000 wood panels covered with paint and stain stand on a farm in New Jersey. The result is acres and acres of every shade of color. By leaving these panels out in each season and all kinds of weather, the company learns how well and how long the paint holds up. Still, as one house painter points out, "No matter how good the paint is, you have to prepare the surface well first."

Choose the answer that best completes each sentence.

1 From this paragraph you can conclude that

Ⓐ yellow is the company's biggest seller.

Ⓑ the company is testing exterior paint.

Ⓒ the company also tests competitors' paint.

Ⓓ the paint panels are changed every month.

2 From the paragraph you **cannot** tell

Ⓐ what the company is hoping to learn.

Ⓑ where the testing grounds are located.

Ⓒ which colors hold up the best outside.

Ⓓ what you have to do first when painting.

Drawing Conclusions

Read the paragraph. Answer the questions.

What does it mean when you toss the salad? Most people think that's when you mix lettuce and dressing together. However, sanitation workers would say that tossing the salad means to throw garbage into the truck. Like workers in many fields, they have their own lingo. A garbage truck is known as a white elephant. Garbage that has been salvaged or saved by someone is called mongo. If a worker's job is to pick up trash from street-corner cans, it is called running the baskets. As for the workers, they call themselves trash hounds.

Choose the answer that best completes each sentence.

1 From this paragraph you can conclude that

   (A) people throw away a lot of salad.

   (B) sanitation workers are fond of dogs.

   (C) elephants are used for collecting garbage.

   (D) lingo gives workers a sense of belonging

2 From the paragraph you **cannot** tell

   (A) what "running the baskets" means.

   (B) there are two meanings for tossing the salad.

   (C) how much garbage a truck collects.

   (D) what salvaged garbage is called.

Drawing Conclusions

Read the paragraph. Answer the questions.

Scientists have been learning more about ears. Until recently, most people thought both ears did the same work. However, studies have now shown that the right and left ear process sound differently. If you are listening to someone speaking, your right ear is responding. If you are listening to music, your left ear is more attuned. Researchers think this new information is important in helping people with hearing loss. For example, a student with hearing loss in the right ear might need more help in school because the right ear is critical to learning situations.

Choose the answer that best completes each sentence.

1 From this paragraph you can conclude that
Ⓐ people really don't need two ears.
Ⓑ the left ear is important to musicians.
Ⓒ the right ear is larger than the left ear.
Ⓓ the left and right ear are interchangeable.

2 From the paragraph you **cannot** tell
Ⓐ how scientists conducted their research.
Ⓑ which ear processes speech best.
Ⓒ who might benefit from this research.
Ⓓ what people used to assume about ears.

Name _____ Date _____

Drawing Conclusions

30

Read the paragraph. Answer the questions.

The Romans had a name for it. They called it "nomen et omen," meaning that names are a person's destiny. In other words, someone's name can determine what that person does. Researchers who study this have come up with some convincing examples. For example, Cecil Fielder was a baseball player for Detroit. William Wordsworth was a famous poet. A well-liked weather reporter on television is Storm Field, and a popular entertainer is Tommy Tune. Larry Speakes was a presidential press secretary. Guess what David J. Lawyer does!

Hello
my name is
Dan Green
Environmentalist

Choose the answer that best completes each sentence.

1 From this paragraph you can conclude that
- (A) everyone named Fish works in oceanography.
- (B) all names relate to people's professions.
- (C) someone named Rose might become a florist.
- (D) a doctor named Kwak is not trustworthy.

2 From the paragraph you cannot tell
- (A) who William Wordsworth was.
- (B) the batting average of Cecil Fielder.
- (C) what "nomen et omen" means.
- (D) what kind of work Storm Field does.

Scholastic Teaching Resources   Inferences & Drawing Conclusions

Drawing Conclusions

Read the paragraph. Answer the questions.

You may have heard about laws passed long ago that seem silly today. Some of these laws are related to the role of women. As women's roles changed over time, the old laws became out-of-date. Many states are working to take such laws off the books. For example, Florida got rid of a law forbidding unmarried women to go parachuting on Sundays. In Maine, it is now legal for women to tickle a man under the chin with a feather duster. Women in Texas no longer face a year in jail for adjusting their stockings in public.

Choose the answer that best completes each sentence.

1 From this paragraph you can conclude that

   Ⓐ laws should be updated from time to time.

   Ⓑ married women are good at parachuting.

   Ⓒ it's rude to tickle people with a feather duster.

   Ⓓ women in Texas stopped wearing stockings.

2 From the paragraph you **cannot** tell

   Ⓐ the reason these laws became out-of-date.

   Ⓑ where it was illegal to adjust stockings in public.

   Ⓒ what happened to the parachuting law in Florida.

   Ⓓ how women felt about the laws when they were made.

Scholastic Teaching Resources   Inferences & Drawing Conclusions

Drawing Conclusions

Read the paragraph. Answer the questions.

When Marco Polo visited China in the thirteenth century, he found many things that were new to him. He was amazed that people in China used paper money. This was unheard of in Europe at that time. Another surprise was the custom of bathing every day. In Europe, baths were taken very rarely. Even more amazing was the "black stone," or coal, used to heat the bath water. The wide streets of the city in which Kublai Khan, China's leader, lived, also impressed Marco Polo. These streets were unlike the twisting, narrow lanes of Italy.

Choose the answer that best completes each sentence.

1 From this paragraph you can conclude that

Ⓐ the Chinese printed their paper money in Europe.

Ⓑ Europeans did not know much about China in the 1200s.

Ⓒ people in the European countries took baths every day.

Ⓓ Marco Polo was a ruler from Italy.

2 From the paragraph you **cannot** tell

Ⓐ that Europeans were unfamiliar with paper money at that time.

Ⓑ what the streets in Italy were like in the thirteenth century.

Ⓒ what people in China found different about Marco Polo.

Ⓓ who the leader of the Chinese was in the 1200s.

Drawing Conclusions

Read the paragraph. Answer the questions.

Many families wash their clothes at public laundromats.
Often, parents must take their children along with the
dirty clothes and pockets of coins when they do the laundry.
To give the children something worthwhile to do while
their parents fold clean clothes, one laundry chain started a
Wash and Learn program. The program operates during
after-school hours and in the evenings. At special tables set up in the laundry,
students can listen to stories, read books by themselves, and get help with their
homework. Several teachers are on hand to help.

Choose the answer that best completes each sentence.

1 From this paragraph you can conclude that

　Ⓐ some students do their homework at school.

　Ⓑ students get grades at the Wash and Learn program.

　Ⓒ the program is helpful to both parents and children.

　Ⓓ the program shows children how to wash clothes.

2 From the paragraph you **cannot** tell

　Ⓐ what the name of the program is.

　Ⓑ what the children do in the program.

　Ⓒ when the program operates.

　Ⓓ how much laundry the parents do.

Drawing Conclusions

Read the paragraph. Answer the questions.

The price for an ice cream cone is posted in a shop window. You decide to buy one. "Would you like a topping?" asks the clerk. You decide to have one. The price of your cone has just gone up. A new word for this practice is *shrouding*. Economists think that shrouding affects much of what people buy today. In a restaurant people pay extra for bottled rather than tap water. A new car has many features that add to its cost. If you buy tickets for an event over the phone, there is an additional charge. How can a consumer avoid shrouding? One answer is to think carefully about the value of things before buying.

**Ice Cream Cones
$1.50—Maybe**

Choose the answer that best completes each sentence.

1 From this paragraph you can conclude that
  (A) all ice cream cones are the same price.
  (B) prices of things are higher than people realize.
  (C) it's better to drink bottled water than tap water.
  (D) it's worthwhile to order tickets over the phone.

2 From the paragraph you **cannot** tell
  (A) how shrouding adds to the price of things.
  (B) where the word *shrouding* came from.
  (C) how the cost of a new car increases.
  (D) why a consumer should think carefully.

Drawing Conclusions

Read the paragraph. Answer the questions.

When a word has been shortened, it is called a clip. For example, a *ref* is a short form of the word *referee*. Over time, many words in English have been clipped. Do you know the original word for a *mike*? It's *microphone*. Something that is a *curio* was once a *curiosity*. You probably enjoy visiting the *zoo*, but at one time people visited a *zoological garden*. Perhaps you go to and from school on a *bus*. Students of the past traveled on an *omnibus*. School words such as *math* and *exams* are simplified versions of *mathematics* and *examinations*.

Choose the answer that best completes each sentence.

1 From this paragraph you can conclude that

Ⓐ it is harder to learn clipped words.

Ⓑ riding on an omnibus was not safe.

Ⓒ clips are easier to pronounce and spell.

Ⓓ people don't like to use short words.

2 From the paragraph you **cannot** tell

Ⓐ the number of clips in the English language.

Ⓑ what the shortened word for *zoological garden* is.

Ⓒ what the word *mike* came from.

Ⓓ how to spell the word *curiosity*.

Making Inferences

Read the paragraph. Answer the questions.

Most people take their autos to a car wash or get out their hose to clean off the dirt and grime. However, one car owner found that a dirty vehicle had its advantages. She parked her car on a city street where a passing driver hit it. The offending motorist drove off without stopping to acknowledge the accident. When the woman found her dented car, she also found a helpful clue about the damage. There, in the mud and frost caked on her very dirty bumper was an imprint of the hit-and-run driver's license plate! The police had no trouble reading the numbers and catching up with the offender.

1 What was the temperature like on the day of the accident? Why do you think so?

_____

2 How do you think the woman probably felt when she found that her car had been hit?

_____

3 How do you think she felt when she saw the imprint of the license plate?

_____

4 How did the police find the offender?

_____

5 How will the woman feel about washing her car in the future?

_____

Drawing Conclusions

Read the paragraph. Answer the questions.

The musk deer is a small hoofed mammal that is found only in Asia. It lives in mountainous areas of forests and brush. These delicate animals weigh about 20 to 25 pounds. The males have small tusks. The musk deer are not easily seen; they come out to graze in the evening darkness or early morning hours. Although their yellowish-brown coloring provides camouflage, the musk deer are heavily hunted. These animals are eagerly sought because they have a gland that produces musk, a waxy substance used to add scent to soaps and perfumes. Scientists have been able to make a synthetic musk, but the real thing is greatly prized.

1 Is it easy to find the musk deer? Explain your answer.

_____

_____

2 How would real musk affect the price of perfume and soap?

_____

_____

3 Why have scientists made a synthetic musk?

_____

_____

4 What conclusion could you make about the future of the musk deer? Why?

_____

_____

Name _____ Date _____

Student Record

Date	Exercise #	Number Correct	Comments

Scholastic Teaching Resources   *Inferences & Drawing Conclusions*

Answers

page 8:
1. preserved bodies of dead as mummies
2. made mummies of their dead kings
3. tried to preserve their emperors in jade suits
4. spent up to 70 days preparing a mummy
My Inference: Answers will vary.

page 9:
1. Corn is grown in many parts of the world.
2. Both people and animals eat corn.
3. Possible: corn cereal, corn chips, and popcorn
4. Possible: tacos and muffins
My Conclusion: Answers will vary.

page 10:
1. Fact, Inference, Fact, Inference 2. yes, yes, no

page 11:
1. Inference, Fact, Inference, Inference 2. yes, no, no

page 12:
1. Inference, Inference, Fact, Inference 2. no, no, yes

page 13:
1. Inference, Fact, Inference, Inference 2. no, yes, yes

page 14:
1. Fact, Inference, Inference, Inference 2. yes, no, no

page 15:
1. Fact, Inference, Inference, Fact 2. yes, no, yes

page 16: 1. Inference, Inference, Fact, Inference
2. no, no, yes

page 17:
1. Inference, Fact, Fact, Fact 2. yes, yes, yes

page 18:
1. Fact, Inference, Fact, Fact 2. yes, no, no

page 19:
1. Inference, Fact, Inference, Fact 2. no, yes, yes

page 20:
1. Inference, Inference, Fact, Inference 2. yes, no, no

page 21:
1. Fact, Fact, Inference, Fact 2. yes, no, yes

page 22:
1. Inference, Inference, Fact, Inference 2. no, yes, no

page 23:
1. Fact, Inference, Fact, Inference 2. yes, no, no

page 24:
1. Fact, Fact, Inference, Inference 2. no, no, yes

page 25:
1. Fact, Inference, Fact, Inference 2. no, no, yes

page 26:
1. Fact, Fact, Fact, Inference 2. no, yes, no

page 27:
1. C 2. A

page 28:
1. D 2. B

page 29:
1. B 2. C

page 30:
1. C 2. D

page 31:
1. A 2. C

page 32:
1. C 2. B

page 33:
1. D 2. B

page 34:
1. B 2. C

page 35:
1. A 2. D

page 36:
1. B 2. C

page 37:
1. D 2. C

page 38:
1. B 2. A

page 39:
1. C 2. B

page 40:
1. A 2. D

page 41:
1. B 2. C

page 42:
1. C 2. D

page 43:
1. B 2. B

page 44:
1. C 2. A

page 45:
Possible:
1. It was cold because there was frost on the bumper.
2. She was probably upset.
3. She might have been surprised and also hopeful.
4. They tracked the offender through the license plate.
5. She might be reluctant because a dirty car was lucky for her.

page 46:
Possible:
1. No, because they come out at dark and are well camouflaged.
2. It would make the price go up.
3. Real musk is not easy to get.
4. They may be endangered because they are hunted.

Scholastic Teaching Resources *Inferences & Drawing Conclusions*